Published By Robert Corbin

@ Sean Turner

Dukan Diet Cookbook: Delicious

Recipes

All Right RESERVED

ISBN 978-87-94477-37-6

TABLE OF CONTENTS

Fruit Chicken Salad 1

Turkey Meatballs With Tomato Sauce 4

Meatball Soup 9

Miso Soup 12

Grilled Eggplant With Mint And Garlic 14

Chicken Salad With Mixed Vegetables 16

Chicken And Vegetable Stew..................................... 17

Chocolate Goji Berry Cookies 19

Salmon And Shrimp Hot Pot...................................... 21

Grapefruit Pie 23

Coconut Smoothie 25

Meatballs With Rosemary 26

Salmon In A Mustard Dill Sauce 28

Eggs Cocotte 30

Pan Seared Shrimp & Browned Zucchini Salad 32

Salmon And Broccoli Tabbouleh 35

Orange Soda Cake 37

Eggplant Soup... 42

Ken's Perfect Hard Boiled Egg 45

Marinara Sauce Yet 47

Tandoori Chicken Fillets 49

Chicken Supreme.. 51

Kale Chips 53

Earthy Kale Salad 55

Zucchini Lasagna... 57

Mocha Chocolate Oat Bran Muffins........................ 60

Basil Thai Chicken 62

Roasted Brussels Sprouts 64

Garlic Shirataki Noodles 66

Shirataki Noodles With Ground Beef, Cherry Tomatoes, And Asparagus... 68

Shirataki Noodles Bolognese.................................... 70

Turkey Meatballs Quickstart Guide.......................... 72

Vinegar Fish 74

Ginger Salmon 76

Unayaki Steak With Tzatziki 77

Eggplant Rolls Stuffed With Ricotta 80

Shrimp And Pineapple Skewers............................... 84

Smoked Salmon With Boiled Eggs And Capers........ 87

Chicken Pasta 89

Salmon Ceviche 91

Cream Of Pumpkin And Carrot Soup....................... 92

Salmon And Cream Cheese Croutons...................... 94

Baked Salmon And Sautéed Spinach With Dijon Cream 95

Fried Egg And Vegetable Skillet 97

Sautéed White Fish In Red Sauce 99

Peach Pecan Pie 103

Oreo Pie 105

Smoked Salmon Appetizers 107

Ham Appetizers 108

Turkey Meatballs Recipe: Dukan Diet Quickstart Guide 110

Healthy Flat Bread 112

Friendly Turkey Meatballs 114

Pita According To Dukan 116

Simple Roasted Butternut Squash 120

Roast Sticky Chickenrotisserie Style 122

- Barbara's Sesame Chicken 124
- Turkey Burgers 126
- Basil Pesto Artichokes 127
- Sautéed Shiitake And Swiss Chard 129
- Cheese And Garlic Chicken Pocket 131
- Pink Cheesecake Cupcake 133
- Lemon Chicken Light 135
- Sticky Chicken 138

Fruit Chicken Salad

Ingredients:

- 1/2 cup white grapes, halved

- 1/4 cup chopped walnuts

- 2 tablespoons of Greek yogurt

- Lemon juice

- Fresh mint, chopped

- 200g chicken breast, cooked and diced

- 1 green apple, diced

- 1 orange, peeled and cut into wedges

- Salt and pepper (to taste).

Directions:

1. Prepare the Chicken Breast: Cook the chicken breast in steam or in salted water until fully cooked. Let it cool, then cut it into cubes.
2. Prepare the fruit: Cut the green apple into cubes and peel the orange, then cut it into wedges. Cut the white grapes in half.
3. Assemble the Salad: In a large bowl, combine the chicken, green apple, orange wedges, white grapes, and chopped walnuts. Stir gently to combine Ingredients:.
4. Make the Salsa: In a small bowl, mix the Greek yogurt with lemon juice, chopped fresh mint, salt, and pepper. Adjust the consistency with a little water if necessary.
5. Dressing: Pour the prepared sauce over the chicken and fruit salad. Stir well to distribute the dressing evenly.
6. Resting: Let the salad rest in the refrigerator for at least 30 minutes to allow the flavors to meld.

7. Service: Transfer fruit chicken salad to a platter. You can garnish with fresh mint leaves and a few chopped walnuts. Serve the salad as an appetizer or as a light main course.
8. Fruit Chicken Salad is a fresh and light option for the Dukan Diet. The combination of chicken, fruit and nuts provides a mix of interesting flavors and textures.
9. You can customize the recipe by adding other fruits of your choice, such as pomegranate or pineapple. Be sure to choose fresh, inseason fruit for maximum flavor.

Turkey Meatballs With Tomato Sauce

Ingredients:

For the meatballs:

- 1 clove of garlic, finely chopped

- 2 tablespoons fresh parsley, chopped

- Salt and pepper (to taste)

- 250g of ground turkey meat

- 1 egg

- 1/4 cup breadcrumbs (or oat bran for the Dukan diet)

- Extra virgin olive oil (for cooking).

For the tomato sauce:

- 2 cloves of garlic, finely chopped

- 1 tablespoon of extra virgin olive oil

- 1 teaspoon dried oregano

- 400g of peeled tomatoes

- 1 onion, finely chopped

- Salt and pepper (to taste).

Directions:

1. Make the meatballs: In a bowl, combine the ground turkey meat, egg, breadcrumbs (or oat bran), minced garlic, fresh parsley, salt, and pepper.
2. Mix the Ingredients: well until you get a homogeneous mixture.
3. Shape the meatballs: Take a portion of the dough and shape into evenly sized meatballs, about 34 inches in diameter. Repeat the process until you run out of dough.
4. Cook the meatballs: In a nonstick pan, heat a little extra virgin olive oil.
5. Arrange the meatballs in the skillet and cook them over mediumhigh heat, turning occasionally, until browned and cooked through (about 10 to 12 minutes). Remove the meatballs from the pan and set them aside.

6. Prepare the tomato sauce: In a saucepan, heat the extra virgin olive oil.
7. Add the chopped onion and minced garlic and cook them until soft and golden brown. Add the peeled tomatoes, dried oregano, salt and pepper.
8. Lightly mash the tomatoes with a fork to break them up. Simmer the sauce over mediumlow heat for about 15 to 20 minutes, until it thickens slightly.
9. Combine the meatballs with the sauce: Add the turkey meatballs to the saucepan with the tomato sauce and cook for another 510 minutes over low heat, so that they absorb the flavors well.
10. Service: Transfer the turkey meatballs with tomato sauce to a platter. You can garnish with some chopped fresh parsley.

11. Serve the meatballs as an appetizer or main course, accompanied by fresh vegetables or a portion of whole grains.
12. Turkey meatballs with tomato sauce are a tasty and proteinrich option for the Dukan diet.
13. The meatballs can be made ahead of time and stored in the refrigerator to be eaten throughout the week.
14. Homemade tomato sauce adds a touch of flavor and filling to the dish.

Meatball Soup

Ingredients:

- Handful of cilantro, chopped
- Handful of scallions, chopped
- 1 tsp salt
- 1 ½ tsp pepper
- 1 tbsp mustard
- 1 tbsp fresh dill, chopped
- 1 tbsp Worcester sauce
- 1 egg white
- 2 cups fatfree chicken broth
- 1/3 cup pork, minced

- 1/3 cup chicken, minced

- ¼ cup oat bran

- 1 clove of garlic, crushed

Directions:

1. In a food processor, blend the eggs, cilantro, scallions, salt, pepper, mustard, dill, Worcester sauce and garlic to combine them. Pulse around 5 times.
2. In a bowl, mix the oat bran and meat together. Then, add the egg mixture to the bowl and combine – knead using your hands.
3. Scoop out the mixture and roll each into a small ball using your hand. Arrange them on a baking sheet and cool it for an hour.
4. Boil the chicken broth then reduce it to a simmer. Put the meatballs into the broth – then reduce the heat further. Let them cook completely this should take around 5 minutes.
5. Garnish with fresh chives and a dash of lemon juice.

Miso Soup

Ingredients:

- ¼ cup miso

- ¼ block of firm tofu

- ½ tbsp nori seaweed, shredded

- 2 cups water

- 1 ½ scallions, finely chopped

- ½ tbsp soy sauce

Directions:

1. In a soup pot, bring the seaweed placed in the water to a simmer – let it remain that way for 5 minutes. (The longer you simmer, the less strong the taste becomes.)

2. Reduce the heat to low. Next, add the scallions, miso, tofu and soy sauce.
3. Keep stirring till the miso dissolves completely.

Grilled Eggplant With Mint And Garlic

Ingredients:

- Fresh mint leaves, finely chopped
- Extra virgin olive oil
- 2 medium eggplants
- 2 garlic cloves, finely chopped
- Salt and pepper to taste.

Directions:

1. Cut the eggplant into lengthwise slices about 1 cm thick. Heat a grill or nonstick skillet over mediumhigh heat.
2. Brush both sides of the eggplant slices with olive oil and sprinkle with salt and pepper.

3. Grill the eggplant slices for about 5 to 7 minutes on each side until they are soft and lightly browned.
4. While the eggplant is grilling, mix the minced garlic and mint in a small bowl with a little olive oil.
5. When ready, remove the eggplant from the grill and brush both sides with the garlic and mint mixture. Arrange the grilled eggplant on a serving platter and serve.

Chicken Salad With Mixed Vegetables

Ingredients:

- Cucumbers, carrots, peppers), diced
- 1 tablespoon light mayonnaise
- Lemon juice
- 200 g cooked and diced chicken breast.
- Mixed vegetables of your choice (e.g., tomatoes,
- Salt and pepper to taste.

Directions:

1. In a bowl, combine the diced chicken breast and mixed vegetables. Add the light mayonnaise and lemon juice.

2. Season with salt and pepper to taste. Gently mix all Ingredients: until evenly mixed. Allow to rest in the refrigerator for a few minutes before serving.

Chicken And Vegetable Stew

Ingredients:

- 2 carrots, peeled and diced
- 1 large clove garlic, peeled and crushed
- 4 ½ c. reducedsodium or sodiumfree vegetable stock
- 23 skinless chicken breasts
- ½ eggplant, peeled and diced
- ¼ butternut pumpkin, peeled and diced
- ½ large onion, peeled and diced

- Salt and pepper to taste

Directions:

1. Place eggplant into colander on top of plate with sides. Sprinkle with salt, and allow to sit and drain for about 20 minutes.
2. Cut the chicken to roughly the same size as the rest of the vegetables, as well.
3. Coat bottom of large pot or dutch oven with olive oil (spray is acceptable).
4. Heat oil over medium heat. Add onions and garlic. Stir until onion softens.
5. Add carrots, stirring often. Rinse eggplant in cold water, and then add to soup.
6. Add veggie stock and cover. Bring to a boil and then turn heat down so that stew is simmering. Allow to cook for 45 minutes.
7. Add chicken and simmer until cooked through, stirring often. Salt and pepper to taste.

Chocolate Goji Berry Cookies

Ingredients:

- 1 tbsp. Goji berries

- 2 tbsp. oat bran

- Pinch of salt

- ¼ c. skim milk

- 1 tbsp. Stevia

- ½ tsp. baking powder

- 1 tsp. lowfat, unsweetened cocoa powder

- 1 ½ tbsp. fromage frais

- 2 tbsp. wheat bran

Directions:

1. Preheat oven to 350°F.
2. Mix all Ingredients: in a large bowl. With a small spoon, form little mounds on a baking sheet about 23 inches apart.
3. Bake for about 2030 minutes or until crunchy.

Salmon And Shrimp Hot Pot

Ingredients:

- 1 tsp. garlic, minced

- 6 oz. shrimp

- 1 c. boiling water

- 1 cube fish stock

- 1 c. fatfree Greek yogurt

- 4 salmon fillet

- 3 tbsp. curry powder

- 1 onion, diced

- 2 tsp. spices and herbs

Directions:

1. Grill salmon until cooked through. In a pan, fry onions, garlic, shrimp, and curry powder (add a splash of water, if necessary).
2. Place stock cube into hot water to dissolve. Add herbs and stock to pan.
3. After 10 minutes, add yogurt, and stir well. In final 5 minutes, add salmon. Serve once salmon is warmed through.

Grapefruit Pie

Ingredients:

- 1 cup brown sugar
- ¼ cup flour
- 56 egg yolks
- Pastry sheets
- 2 cups grapefruit
- 5 oz. Butter

Directions:

1. Line a pie plate or pie form with pastry and cover the edges of the plate depending on your preference
2. In a bowl combine all pie Ingredients: together and mix well

3. Pour the mixture over the pastry
4. Bake at 400-425 F for 25-30 minutes or until golden brown
5. When ready remove from the oven and let it rest for 15 minutes

Coconut Smoothie

Ingredients:

- 1 cup pineapple juice
- 2 tablespoons coconut flakes
- ½ cup yogurt
- 2 cup pineapple
- ¼ cup coconut milk
- 1 tablespoon honey

Directions:

1. In a blender place all Ingredients: and blend until smooth
2. Pour smoothie in a glass and serve

Meatballs With Rosemary

Ingredients:

- 1 egg, lightly beaten
- 2 tbsp Chinese plum sauce
- 1 tbsp Worcestershire sauce
- 2 tbsp rosemary, finely chopped
- 1–2 tbsp mint or basil, finely chopped
- 1 medium onion, chopped
- 750g (1lb 10oz) minced beef
- 2 garlic cloves, crushed
- Salt and black pepper

Directions:

1. Mix together all the ingredient and then shape into meatballs the size of a walnut.
2. Cook the meatballs, a few at a time, in a saucepan over a medium heat for about five minutes until they are goldenbrown on all sides.
3. Allow any fat to drain off on to kitchen paper.

Salmon In A Mustard Dill Sauce

Ingredeints:

- 1 tbsp mild mustard

- 6 tsp virtually fatfree fromage frais

- Finely chopped dill

- 4 thick pieces of salmon, weighing around 200g (7oz) each

- 2 shallots, chopped

- Salt and black pepper

Directions:

1. Put salmon in the freezer for a few minutes so you can cut it into thin 50g (1¾ oz) slices then fry in a nonstick frying pan for one minute on each side. Remove and keep warm.

2. Brown the shallots in the same frying pan, cover with the mustard and fromage frais and allow to thicken for five minutes over a gentle heat.
3. Return salmon to the pan with dill, salt and pepper for a few seconds, then serve.

Eggs Cocotte

Ingredients:

- 2 slices of smoked salmon (ham or bresaola)

- 6 eggs

- 12 tsp virtually fatfree fromage frais

- Tarragon (or chervil), chopped

- Salt and black pepper

Directions:

1. Put 2 tsp of the fromage frais and a pinch of herbs into each of six ramekin dishes.
2. Add a third of a slice of smoked salmon, cut into fine strips, then one egg and salt and pepper.
3. Place ramekin dishes in a highsided saucepan filled with boiling water like a bainmarie.

Cover and cook for 3–5 minutes over a medium heat.

Pan Seared Shrimp & Browned Zucchini Salad

Ingredients:

- 10 shrimps (peeled, keep the ends)

- pinch of salt

- 3/4 cup arugula salad

- 1/3 cup + 1/3 cup water

- 1 cup chopped yellow zucchini

- 1/2 tsp olive oil

For the salad dressing:

- 1/4 tsp salt

- 1 sachet sweetener

- 1/2 lemon (juiced)

- 1 oz (30 g) fatfree Greek yogurt

- 1 tsp mustard

- 1 tsp warm water

Directions:

1. Combine ingredients for salad dressing in a bowl and whisk until wellmixed.
2. Pour 1/3 cup of water into a large nonstick skillet, then add in chopped zucchini.
3. Cook the zucchini with water over medium heat, until water, has evaporated and zucchini lightly stick to the pan, stirring occasionally.
4. Add in more water (about 1/3 cup) and repeat the same until the zucchini is browned to your liking. Add the browned zucchini to the salad dressing.
5. Preheat olive oil in a nonstick skillet.
6. Lightly coat the shrimps with salt, then cook in a single layer until turned pink.

7. Turn the shrimps and continue cooking until just cooked through.
8. Add the shrimp and arugula to the zucchini and toss to mix well.

Salmon And Broccoli Tabbouleh

Ingredients:

- Small handful parsley, chopped

- Small handful mint, chopped 2 spring onions, trimmed and sliced

- Grated zest of ½ lime

- 1 salmon fillet

- 2 tablespoons oat bran

- 1/3 cup broccoli florets

- Seasoning (salt and pepper to taste)

Directions:

1. Place the oat bran in a bowl and pour over 2 tablespoons boiling water and leave to stand for 10 minutes.
2. Sream or blanch the broccoli in boiling water then refresh under cold running water.
3. Fluff the oat bran with a fork then stir in the chopped herbs, spring onion, lime zest, broccoll and seasoning.
4. Grill the salmon fillet to your liking and serve with the tabbouleh.
5. Alternatively you could flake the fish and stir into the tabbouleh to serve.

Orange Soda Cake

Ingredients:

- 150 ml. orange flavored sugar free sodasuitable mineral water with gas

- 1 tsp baking powder10 gr

- Spicescinnamon, ginger, nutmeg, red pepper to taste

- A pinch of salt

- For glaze

- Skimmed milk as needed0.5%1.5%

- 45 tbsp skimmed milk powder (SOM)60 gr   2 DOPs

- 2 tbsp cornstarch 40 gr(2 DOPs)

- 4 tbsp oat bran60 gr

- 3 eggs not very large

- 30 gr glutencan be replaced with isolate

- 1 tbsp orange peel

- sucrose

Directions:

1. The Directions: of Dukan's orange cake is quite simple.
2. First, peel the zest from an orange with a special knife or fine grater.
3. We use only the colored part of the zest, we do not touch the white part it is bitter
4. Separate eggs into whites and yolks
5. Add yolks and zest to dry Ingredients:, pour in soda

6. IMPORTANT! Soda must be highly carbonated! If you use mineral water also do not release gas in advance
7. It is necessary to use soda without sugar, only on permitted sweeteners! The energy value should not exceed 1 Kcal. If you think soda is basically harmful, just skip this recipe =)
8. Beat with a mixer until smooth
9. Beat egg whites using a pinch of salt until stiff peaks form. There should be a spoon in the proteins until such a state we need to beat them
10. Gently fold your beaten egg whites into the batter, using gentle movements so that they don't fall off.
11. We choose the appropriate form. You can use a special cupcake, or you can take a form for bread
12. Bake at 180 C for like 2530 minutes until "dry sticks"

13. Preferably in topdown mode, without convection.
14. Leave in the switched off oven for another 5 minutes. Then we get it right away. Lay out on the grill
15. While our Dukan cake is cooling down a bit, let's do the icing.
16. Mix a few tablespoons of liquid milk with dry. Add sugar.
17. Mix the glaze until smooth, so that there are no lumps.
18. Better to do it with a mixer. If necessary, add a little more liquid or powdered milk.
19. While still warm, drizzle generously with frosting.
20. Let the cake cool down completely. During this time, the glaze will harden.
21. When serving, you can sprinkle with powdered sweetener or SOM

22. The cake turns out fluffy, moist and very fragrant! Try!

Eggplant Soup

Ingredients:

- 1 medium onion

- 1 st. l. balsamic vinegarrice/apple/wine

- fresh or dried thymeProvence herbs can be used

- salt, pepper to taste

- 1 tsp olive oilif it is needed

- 600 gr. fresh eggplant

- 1 medium bell pepper

- 500 ml drinking water

- 2 garlic cloves

Directions:

1. We clean the eggplants from the skin, cut into mediumsized pieces and pour a small amount of water for 1520 minutes. After the time has elapsed, drain the water.
2. Fry eggplant on all sides in a nonstick frying pan without oil until golden brown. Pour in vinegar, add thyme (if the thyme is fresh, you need to pick off the leaves from the branches) or seasonings, keep a little more on the stove. We take it off the fire.
3. Finely chop the onion. Let's skip the garlic through the press. Finely chop the pepper.
4. In a saucepan using a thick bottom, heat 1 tsp. olive oil if necessary (you can fry without oil), fry onion and garlic until soft over low heat. Add pepper and fry for a couple more minutes.
5. Add fried eggplants to a saucepan, pour in drinking water.

6. Bring to a boil with simmer covered over low heat for 20 minutes.
7. Remove soup from heat with puree with an immersion blender. If the soup is so thick, you can add a little more water.
8. Salt, pepper and keep the soup on fire for a couple of minutes.
9. Serve with fresh thyme and enjoy! Can be served with crackers, for example from this bread
10. Delicious and fragrant Dukan soup. Try!

Ken's Perfect Hard Boiled Egg

Ingredients:

- ¼ cup distilled white vinegar
- 6 cups water
- 1 tablespoon salt
- 8 eggs

Directions:

1. Combine the salt, vinegar, and water in a large pot, and bring to a boil over high heat.
2. Add the eggs one at a time, being careful not to crack them. Reduce the heat to a gentle boil, and cook for 14 minutes.
3. Once the eggs have cooked, remove them from the hot water, and place into a container of ice water or cold, running water.

4. Cool completely, about 15 minutes. Store in the refrigerator up to 1 week.

Marinara Sauce Yet

Ingredients:

- 1 teaspoon dried oregano

- 1 teaspoon salt

- ¼ teaspoon ground black pepper

- 6 tablespoons olive oil

- ⅓ cup finely diced onion

- 2 (14.5 ounce) cans stewed tomatoes

- 1 (6 ounce) can tomato paste

- 4 tablespoons chopped fresh parsley

- 1 clove garlic, minced

- ½ cup white wine

Directions:

1. In a food processor place Italian tomatoes, tomato paste, chopped parsley, minced garlic, oregano, salt, and pepper. Blend until smooth.
2. In a large skillet over medium heat saute the finely chopped onion in olive oil for 2 minutes. Add the blended tomato sauce and white wine.
3. Simmer for 30 minutes, stirring occasionally.

Tandoori Chicken Fillets

Ingredients:

- 2 tablespoons Zero fat Yogurt

- Juice from one Lemon

- 1 Green Chilli

- 1 Garlic Clove

- 2 Skinless Chicken Breast Fillets

- 2 tablespoons Tandoori Masala Spice Mix

- 1cm piece Peeled Ginger

Directions:

1. Finely dice the chilli, ginger and garlic glove and place in pestle and mortar with the masals spice mix and lemon juice.

2. Grind to a smooth paste.
3. Place yogurt in a bowl and stir in the paste to complete the marinade.
4. Score each breast 2 or 3 times to help it absorb the flavors (or cut chicken breast into goujons or cubes).
5. Place the chicken in the bowl and cover well with the marinade.
6. Put cling film over the bowl and place in the refrigerator overnight.
7. Bake, grill or barbecue making sure that the meat is thoroughly cooked.
8. Serve with a little zero fat yogurt.

Chicken Supreme

Ingredients:

- 2 teaspoon of Dijon Mustard
- 2 tablespoons of Fat Free Yogurt
- 2 teaspoon of Chopped Chives
- 2 Chicken Breast
- 1 glass of White Wine (Tolerated)
- Salt and Pepper to taste

Directions:

1. Cut the chicken breast into strips and dry fry in a pan for one minute to seal.
2. Add the white wine and continue cooking until the chicken is done.

3. In a bowl mix the remaining ingredients to make the sauce.
4. Allow the chicken to cool slightly before adding the sauce and then serve.

Kale Chips

Ingredients:

- 1 tbsp extra virgin olive oil

- 1 bunch Kale

- Sea salt to taste

- 1 tbsp sherry vinegar

Directions:

1. Grease baking sheet, and preheat oven to 300oF.
2. Prepare kale leaves by cutting out the ribs and discarding.
3. Wash torn kale, and dry thoroughly.
4. Place on baking sheet, and season with salt, vinegar, and oil.

5. Spread kale evenly on baking sheet, and pop into the oven.
6. Bake for 35 minutes, or until kale is crispy.
7. Serve right away, and enjoy!

Earthy Kale Salad

Ingredients:

- ½ cup tamari soy sauce

- ½ cup lemon juice

- ½ cup chopped fresh dill

- 1 cup chopped fresh flat leaf parsley

- ½ large head red cabbage, chopped

- 1 bunch kale, ribs removed, chopped

- Pepper and salt to taste

- ¼ cup stone ground mustard

- 8 cloves garlic chopped

- 2 tbsp extravirgin olive oil

Directions:

1. In a big bowl, mix together dill, parsley, red cabbage, kale, and sesame seeds.
2. In a separate and smaller bowl, mix together mustard, garlic, olive oil, soy sauce, and lemon juice, and whisk thoroughly together.
3. Pour into bowl of salad until desired taste is reached. Toss salad, and add more sauce if needed.
4. Serve, and enjoy!

Zucchini Lasagna

Ingredients:

- 3 1/2 oz. Of turkey bosom, smoked

- 3 1/2 oz. Of mozzarella cheddar, light

- 1 tbsp. Of tomato separate, pure

- 1/2 onion, medium

- 1 garlic clove

- 2 lengthwayscut zucchinis, medium

- 2 stripped, decultivated tomatoes, ready, large

- 7 ounces of ground hamburger, lean

- as wanted: oregano, chives, parsley, fit salt and

- Ground pepper

Directions:

1. Grill each side of cut zucchinis in nonstick dish. Set aside.
2. Sauté onion and garlic in dish on low hotness. Add legitimate salt, ground pepper and meat. Cook on low.
3. Pour 1 3/4 fl. oz. of separated water in food processor. Add chives, parsley and tomatoes (diced). Consolidate till smooth.
4. Add sauce to meat. Add tomato extricate. Bubble blend for 1215 minutes.
5. Add some sauce to baking dish/pizza structure for stove cooking. Structure layers utilizing zucchini, then, at that point, turkey bosom, then, at that point, cheddar and sauce. Rehash layers twice. Top with cheddar and oregano.

6. Place in broiler for 2025 minutes. Then, at that point, go broiler to off. Permit lasagna to sit for 1215 minutes. Serve.

Mocha Chocolate Oat Bran Muffins

Ingredients:

- Bob's Red Mill High Fiber Oat Bran Hot Cereal (1/3 cup dry, 1 cup prepared), 1.50 cup (remove)

- Cocoa, dry powder, unsweetened, 0.25 cup (remove)

- Egg, fresh, 5 large (remove)

- Yogurt, Stonyfield Farm fat free plain (6 oz), 0.75 cup (remove)

- Splenda, 24 tsp (remove)

- Vanilla Extract, 1 tsp (remove)

- baking powder, 4 tsp (remove)

- 1/2 tsp. salt

- 1/4 tsp. espresso powder

Directions:

1. Preheat oven to 350. Prepare a muffin tin using paper muffin cups, then spray the paper cups with baking spray or coconut oil spray.
2. Mix together all dry ingredients (oat bran, cocoa powder, Splenda, Stevia, baking powder, espresso powder and salt) in a medium bowl.
3. Beat eggs in a large bowl until frothy, then add yogurt and vanilla and mix until creamy.
4. Add in dry ingredients and mix until combined. Fill muffin cups 2/3 full. Bake for 18 minutes or until a cake tester comes out clean.

Basil Thai Chicken

Ingredients:

- 6 chopped, pounded bird (Thai) chilies

- 2 eggs, large

- ½ lb. cubed chicken, boneless

- 2 diced shallots

- 1 tbsp. fish sauce, Thai

- 4 minced garlic cloves

- 1 pinch pepper, white

- Large bunch stemremoved Thai basil, sweet

- 2 slivered lime leaves, kaffir

- 3 tsp. soy sauce, sweet, black

- Nonstick spray

- 2 tsp. Splenda

Directions:

1. Spray heated skillet, then add shallots and garlic. Stir fry them till they are aromatic.
2. Add chicken meat. Stir fry quickly. Break chicken meat into small sized lumps.
3. When chicken has changed color, add chilies and seasonings. Continue stirfrying.
4. Add basil leaves. Stir a few times till basil leaves wilt and you smell their exotic fragrance.
5. Sprinkle 2 dashes of white pepper powder in mixture. Stir one last time. Transfer to dishes. Serve promptly.

Roasted Brussels Sprouts

Ingredients:

- 2 tsp. honey, organic
- 3 tbsp. oil, olive
- 1 ½ lb. Brussels sprouts, frozen
- ¼ tsp. pepper, black
- 2 tbsp. vinegar, balsamic
- ½ tsp. salt, kosher

Directions:

1. Preheat the oven to 425F. Line a large sized cookie sheet with baking paper.
2. Trim ends from Brussels sprouts. Peel off any wilted leaves and toss them.

3. Arrange the Brussels sprouts on a cookie sheet. Use oil to drizzle. Season using kosher salt and ground pepper.
4. Toss and coat the sprouts evenly. Spread them out into one layer with no pieces overlapping.
5. Roast the Brussels sprouts for 1520 minutes, till the edges are caramelized. Remove them from the oven.
6. Whisk vinegar and honey together in a small sized bowl. Pour this mixture over the roasted Brussels sprouts. Evenly coat by tossing and serve promptly.

Garlic Shirataki Noodles

Ingredients:

- 4 tomatoes, very finely chopped

- 1 red bell pepper, stem and seeds removed, finely chopped

- 1 green bell pepper, stem and seeds removed, finely chopped

- 1 yellow bell pepper, stem and seeds removed, finely chopped

- 1 tablespoon capers, drained and rinsed

- 1 teaspoon caper brine

- tablespoons white wine vinegar

- 3 tablespoons Vinaigrette Maya

- 2 garlic cloves, chopped

- Salt and freshly ground black pepper

- 2 (7ounce) packages of shirataki noodles, such as Dukan Diet Shirataki Noodles, prepared according to the

Directions:

1. In a large bowl, thoroughly combine the vinegar, vinaigrette, and garlic, plus salt and black pepper to taste.
2. Add the tomatoes, bell peppers, capers, and caper brine.
3. Place the prepared shirataki noodles in a large bowl, top with the tomato mixture, and add salt and pepper to taste.

Shirataki Noodles With Ground Beef, Cherry Tomatoes, And Asparagus

Ingredients:

- 3 ounces cherry tomatoes (about 15), cut in half

- 12 spears of asparagus, cut into 44inch pieces

- 2 (7ounce) packages of shirataki noodles, such as Dukan Diet Shirataki Noodles, prepared according to the

- ⅛ teaspoon vegetable oil

- 1 onion, chopped

- 1 pound 95% lean ground beef

- Salt and freshly ground black pepper

Directions:

1. Heat a large nonstick skillet over medium heat. Add the oil, and wipe out any excess with a paper towel.
2. Add the onion to the pan and cook, stirring often, for 5 to 6 minutes.
3. Add the ground beef and season with salt and pepper to taste.
4. Cook, stirring constantly, until browned, about 5 minutes.
5. Add the tomatoes and asparagus. Cook, stirring constantly, until the asparagus is tender, about 5 minutes.
6. Add the prepared noodles and cook, stirring constantly, for an additional 3 minutes.

Shirataki Noodles Bolognese

Ingredients:

- ½ teaspoon finely chopped fresh thyme

- ½ teaspoon finely chopped fresh oregano

- 1 dried bay leaf

- Salt and freshly ground black pepper

- 1 pound 95% lean ground beef

- 2 tomatoes, roughly chopped or 1 cup lowsodium beef stock

- 1 garlic clove, finely chopped

- 1 onion, finely diced

- 1 carrot, finely diced

- 1 stalk of celery, peeled and sliced

- 2 (7ounce) packages of shirataki noodles, such as Dukan Diet Shirataki Noodles, prepared according to the

Directions:

1. Place a large nonstick skillet over low heat, and add 3 tablespoons of water and the garlic and onion. Cook until soft, about 2 minutes.
2. Add the carrot, celery, thyme, oregano, and bay leaf, plus salt and pepper to taste, and cook for an additional 10 minutes.
3. Add the beef and cook, stirring constantly, until browned, about 5 minutes.
4. Add the tomatoes or beef stock, bring to a boil, reduce the heat to a simmer, season with salt and pepper to taste, and cook for 1 hour.
5. Add the prepared noodles to the sauce and cook until heated thoroughly, about 5 minutes. Remove the bay leaf before serving.

Turkey Meatballs Quickstart Guide

Ingredients:

- 2 egg whites, beaten

- 1/2 c. Nonfat cottage cheese

- 1/4 c. Oat bran

- 1/2 c. Fresh mint, minced

- 1 tsp. Dried oregano

- 680 grams. Ground turkey (organic, if possible)

- 1 medium onion, grated

- 2 cloves garlic, minced

- Salt and pepper to taste

Directions:

1. Combine all the ingredients in a mediumsized bowl. Do not overmix or your meatballs can become tough.
2. Scoop out one tablespoon of mixture for each meatball and place formed meatballs on a parchment lined baking sheet.
3. Broil meatballs until browned, turning once.

Vinegar Fish

Ingredients:

- 1 onion, sliced
- 10 whole Allspice
- 150 ml vinegar
- Salt, as needed
- Stevia equivalent to 20 teaspoons of sugar
- Thyme, for tasting and
- 1 ½ kilos fish fillet
- 1 bay leaf
- Vegeta, for tasting.

Directions:

1. Use the ground pepper, salt and thyme to sprinkle over your preferred fish fillet then cover it with onion slices to sit for 2 hours. After 2 hours, set aside the onion slices used to cover the fish for later use.
2. Boil the vegeta and water to cook quickly cook the fish for 2 to 3 minutes and when done, place the fish fillet in a bowl and layer again with the onion slices.
3. In a pot of choice with water, put the allspice and bay leaf and boil. Mix in 1 ½ tablespoons of salt, the sweetener and vinegar to the water and stir.
4. Turn off the heat and while still hot, pour over the onion slicescovered fish fillet in the bowl, cover and let it cool before enjoying. Best enjoyed the day after.

Ginger Salmon

Ingredients:

- 1 ½ tablespoons oat bran

- 1 ginger for tasting, chopped

- 1 salmon and

- Tamari soy sauce for tasting.

Directions:

1. While preheating your oven to 392 degrees F, line a baking tray with foil and lay the salmon on it, topped with ginger slices to taste. Sprinkle soy sauce as well as 1 ½ tablespoons of oat bran.
2. Cover the salmon with the foil and bake in the preheated oven for more or less 25 minutes. To add a somewhat crunchy crust for the

salmon, open the foil covering within the last 5 minutes of baking.

Unayaki Steak With Tzatziki

Ingredients:

- 2 tuna steaks

For the marinade:

- Black pepper and

- Juice of 1 lime.

- 2 tablespoons of readymade teriyaki sauce

For the tzatziki:

- 2 tablespoons fresh dill, chopped

- 250 grams 0% fat Greek yogurt

- Juice of half a lemon and

- 1/3 of a cucumber, deseeded and roughly chopped

- ½ clove of garlic, crushed

- Salt and pepper.

Directions:

1. Combine the lime juice and readymade teriyaki sauce in a shallow bowl. Place the tuna steaks in it and coat with the marinade. With a cling film, cover the bowl and place in the fridge to marinate for at least 30 minutes.
2. As the tuna is absorbing the delicious flavors of the readymade teriyaki sauce and lime juice, use a food processor to blend together the cucumber, garlic, lemon juice and dill until smooth.
3. Pour the cucumber mixture in bowl and mix in the Greek yogurt, stirring until well

incorporated. When done, cover the bowl with cling film and refrigerate.
4. Spray a nonstick pan with some vegetable oil spray, heat it and cook the marinated tuna steaks in it until your desired doneness is achieved.
5. When done, enjoy with the chilled tzatziki dip.

Eggplant Rolls Stuffed With Ricotta

Ingredients:

- 1 egg
- 2 tablespoons fresh parsley, chopped
- Salt and pepper (to taste)
- 400g of tomato sauce
- 2 medium eggplants
- 200g of ricotta
- 2 tablespoons of grated cheese (preferably light)
- Extra virgin olive oil (for cooking).

Directions:

1. Prepare the eggplants: Cut the ends of the eggplants and slice them lengthwise, obtaining thin slices of about half a centimetre. Salt them lightly and let them rest for 1520 minutes on a plate, so that they can lose any excess water.
2. Rinse the eggplants: Rinse the eggplant slices under running water and gently pat them dry with paper towels to remove excess salt and moisture.
3. Eggplant Cotta: Heat a grill or nonstick skillet over mediumhigh heat. Lightly brush the eggplant slices with extra virgin olive oil on both sides. Cook the eggplant slices on the grill or skillet for about 23 minutes per side, until soft and lightly browned. Remove them from the grill or skillet and set them aside.
4. Prepare the filling: In a bowl, mix the ricotta, the grated cheese, the egg, the chopped fresh parsley, salt and pepper. Mix the Ingredients:

well until you get a creamy and homogeneous filling.

5. Eggplant Filling: Take a slice of grilled eggplant and place a teaspoon of ricotta filling on one end.
6. Roll the eggplant slice around the filling, forming a roll. Repeat process with remaining eggplant slices and stuffing.
7. Cooking the rolls: Preheat the oven to 180°C. Arrange the eggplant rolls in a lightly greased baking tray with extra virgin olive oil.
8. Pour the tomato sauce on top of the rolls. Cover the pan with aluminum foil and bake the rolls in the oven for about 2530 minutes, or until the filling is hot and the tomato sauce is just simmering.
9. Service: Transfer the eggplant rolls stuffed with ricotta to a serving plate. You can garnish with some chopped fresh parsley. Serve the

rolls as an appetizer or main course, accompanied by a fresh green salad.

10. Ricottafilled eggplant rolls are a tasty and light option to enrich your Dukan diet. You can customize the recipe by adding spices or herbs to the filling to vary the flavor.

Shrimp And Pineapple Skewers

Ingredients:

- Lemon juice (from half a lemon)
- Salt and pepper (to taste)
- Sweet paprika (optional)
- 2 spoons of extra virgin olive oil
- 200g of fresh, peeled and cleaned prawns
- 200g fresh pineapple, cut into cubes
- 46 wooden toothpicks.

Directions:

1. Shrimp Marinade: In a bowl, add the shrimp, lemon juice, salt, pepper, and sweet paprika (if desired).

2. Stir well to distribute the spices evenly over the shrimp. Let it marinate for about 1520 minutes to allow the flavors to develop.
3. Preparing the skewers: Take a wooden toothpick and thread a prawn followed by a pineapple cube.
4. Continue alternating the shrimp and pineapple until the toothpick is full. Repeat the process with the other toothpicks until you run out of shrimp and pineapple.
5. Cooking the kebabs: Heat a grill or nonstick skillet over mediumhigh heat. Brush the skewers with extra virgin olive oil on both sides to prevent them from sticking to the cooking surface.
6. Place the skewers on the grill or skillet and cook them for about 2 to 3 minutes per side, or until the shrimp are pink and cooked through.

7. Service: Transfer the shrimp and pineapple skewers to a serving platter and drizzle with a squeeze of fresh lemon juice.
8. You can accompany the kebabs with a yogurtbased sauce or light soy sauce if you want to add a touch of extra flavor.
9. Shrimp and pineapple skewers are a light and tasty appetizer, perfect for the Dukan diet. They are rich in protein and fresh fruit, making the dish balanced and nutritious.

Smoked Salmon With Boiled Eggs And Capers

Ingredients:

- 1 tablespoon of capers
- Lemon juice (from half a lemon)
- Ground black pepper (to taste)
- 100g of smoked salmon
- 2 boiled eggs
- Fresh chives (for garnish, optional).

Directions:

1. Directions: of hardboiled eggs: In a saucepan, bring water to a boil. Gently add the eggs and cook them for about 810 minutes.

2. Transfer the eggs to a bowl of cold water to stop cooking. Shell the hardboiled eggs and cut them in half for serving.
3. Directions: of the salmon: Arrange the slices of smoked salmon on a serving plate. You can cut them into thin strips or leave them whole, to your liking.
4. Garnish: Drizzle lemon juice over smoked salmon. Arrange the hardboiled eggs halved on top of the salmon. Distribute the capers on the plate, spreading them evenly.
5. Seasoning: Add a grind of black pepper over the salmon and roe for a kick of flavor.
6. Final Garnish: If you like, you can finely chop some fresh chives and sprinkle them over the dish for an added garnish.
7. Smoked salmon with boiled eggs and capers is a delicious and proteinrich appetizer, perfect for the Dukan diet. You can serve it as an appetizer or as a light main course.

8. Make sure you choose high quality smoked salmon to get the best flavor.

Chicken Pasta

Ingredients:

- ½ onion, finely chopped

- ½ clove of garlic, finely chopped

- 2 tbsp fatfree fromage frais

- 1 cup water

- 1 pack of Shirataki flat noodles

- 2 chicken drumsticks, skinless and boneless, baked and chopped

- Salt, to taste

- Pepper, to taste

Directions:

1. Add the water to the baking dish (with the cooking juices) and pour this into a pan, after removing the excess fat.
2. Boil and reduce it to half its quantity.
3. Cook the onion and garlic in this, till they become soft.
4. Wash the noodles then partboil them and drain the excess water.
5. To the oniongarlic mixture, add chicken, fromage frais, salt and pepper.
6. Next, add the noodles and keep stirring till it cooks completely.

Salmon Ceviche

Ingredients:

- 2 salmons, frozen

- 4 limes

- 8 tbsp dill

- 4 tbsp scallions, minced

- 2 red chilies, seeded and finely diced

Directions:

1. Cut the salmon into cubes of ½ inch each.
2. Use the juice and zest (from the limes) on the salmons, along with the chilies.
3. Cover using cling wrap, and refrigerate for 34 hours.
4. Toss the cubes along with dill and scallions.

Cream Of Pumpkin And Carrot Soup

Ingredients:

- 1 small onion, finely chopped
- 1 clove of garlic, finely chopped
- Vegetable broth to taste
- Salt and pepper to taste
- 300 g pumpkin, cut into cubes
- 2 medium carrots, cut into rounds
- Extra virgin olive oil

Directions:

1. In a saucepan, heat some olive oil and add the chopped onion and garlic.
2. Sauté over medium heat until they turn golden brown. Add the squash, carrots, and

enough vegetable broth to cover the vegetables.
3. Bring to a boil and then reduce to mediumlow heat. Let cook for about 15 to 20 minutes, or until vegetables are soft.
4. Using an immersion blender or mixer, blend the vegetables until smooth.
5. Add extra vegetable broth if needed to achieve the desired consistency.
6. Adjust salt and pepper to suit your taste. Serve the pumpkin and carrot cream hot and garnish with a drizzle of extra virgin olive oil.

Salmon And Cream Cheese Croutons

Ingredients:

- Fresh cheese (e.g., cottage cheese, spreadable cheese)
- Slices of smoked salmon
- Slices of whole wheat bread or toast

Directions:

1. Spread a generous amount of cream cheese on the bread slices.
2. Layer a slice of smoked salmon on top of each crouton.
3. If you wish, you can garnish with fresh dill or chopped parsley for added flavor and decoration. Serve the salmon and cream cheese croutons as an appetizer.

Baked Salmon And Sautéed Spinach With Dijon Cream

Ingredients:

- 1 tsp. Dijon mustard

- ½ c. fatfree sour cream

- Garlic powder to taste

- 2 6-8 oz pieces salmon

- Salt and pepper to taste

- ½ c. 99% fatfree chicken broth

- 1 c. baby spinach

- Parsley, chopped to taste

- Scallions to taste

Directions:

1. Preheat oven to 350°F.
2. Place salmon on baking tray, skin side down, and bake in oven. In a small saucepan, simmer mustard, seasonings, and chicken broth. In another pan, sauté spinach in a pan with water.
3. When salmon is cooked through, remove dijon mixture form heat and add sour cream. Whisk until smooth. Serve sauce on top of salmon and spinach.

Fried Egg And Vegetable Skillet

Ingredients:

- ½ tsp. oregano

- ½ tsp. sweet paprika

- 7 oz canned tomatoes, chopped

- 2 eggs

- ½ a bell pepper (red or yellow)

- 1 onion, sliced thinly

- ¼ tsp. chili powder (optional)

- ½ tsp. ground cumin

- Handful fresh cilantro, chopped

Directions:

1. Sauté onion in a nonstick frying pan until it starts to brown. Add peppers, spices, and herbs. Sauté until fragrant.
2. Add tomatoes, salt, pepper and cook on low heat for 5 minutes. Add extra water if starting to darken too much.
3. Make 2 Hollows In Your Veggies And Carefully Crack One Egg Into Each One. Turn Up Heat And Cook Eggs To Your Preference. Garnish With Fresh Cilantro.

Sautéed White Fish In Red Sauce

Ingredients:

- Zest of 1 lemon

- 1 small onion, sliced finely

- 1 tbsp. fresh parsley, chopped

- 1 red pepper, finely sliced

- 1 tsp. sweet paprika

- 7 oz canned tomato, chopped

- ½ tsp. turmeric

- ¼ tsp. chili powder

- 1 tbsp. fresh cilantro, chopped

- 2 garlic cloves, crushed

- ½ tsp, ground cumin

- 3 tbsp. lemon juice

- 14 oz firm white fish

Directions:

1. Mix all marinade Ingredients: together in bowl (sweet paprika, ground cumin, 1 clove crushed garlic, lemon juice, 1 tbsp each fresh chopped parsley and coriander, salt and pepper).
2. Place fish in a single layer inside a casserole dish, and sprinkle evenly with marinade.
3. Allow to marinate at least 2 hours. coat the fish in the marinade. Leave to marinade for a minimum of 2 hours, or overnight.
4. Preheat oven to 350°F.
5. Sauté onion in a nonstick frying pan until tender. Add garlic, lemon zest and spices. Cook for 2 minutes.
6. Add garlic, lemon zest and spices and cook for 2 minutes. Add red pepper and chopped canned tomatoes.
7. Bring mixture to a simmer, and cook gently for 5 minutes. Salt and pepper to taste.

8. Spread the sauce evenly over the fish and bake in the oven for 20 minutes, or until the fish cab be flaked with a fork.

Peach Pecan Pie

Ingredients:

- 4 small egg yolks

- ¼ Cup flour

- 1 tsp vanilla extract

- 45 cups peaches

- 1 tablespoon preserves

- 1 cup sugar

Directions:

1. Line a pie plate or pie form with pastry and cover the edges of the plate depending on your preference
2. In a bowl combine all pie Ingredients: together and mix well

3. Pour the mixture over the pastry
4. Bake at 400-425 F for 25-30 minutes or until golden brown
5. When ready remove from the oven and let it rest for 15 minutes

Oreo Pie

Ingredients:

- 1 cup halfandhalf
- 1 package instant pudding mix
- 1012 oreo cookies
- Pastry sheets
- 68 oz. Chocolate crumb piecrust
- 10 oz. Whipped topping

Directions:

1. Line a pie plate or pie form with pastry and cover the edges of the plate depending on your preference
2. In a bowl combine all pie Ingredients: together and mix well

3. Pour the mixture over the pastry
4. Bake at 400425 F for 2530 minutes or until golden brown
5. When ready remove from the oven and let it rest for 15 minutes

Smoked Salmon Appetizers

Ingredients:

- 1 small jar of salmon roe
- Salt and black pepper
- 300g (10½ oz) virtually fatfree fromage frais
- 60g (2¼ oz) virtually fatfree quark
- 4 slices of smoked salmon

Directions:

1. Beat together fromage frais and quark. Fold in the salmon roe, salt and pepper.
2. Place a little of this mixture on to each slice of salmon and roll up, securing with a knotted chive or cocktail stick. Eat with mini pancakes.

Ham Appetizers

Ingredients:

- A few chives, finely chopped
- 4 shallots, finely chopped
- Marjoram (or another herb, depending on your taste), finely chopped
- 175g (6oz) extralean ham, chopped
- 225g (8oz) virtually fatfree quark
- A few drops of Tabasco

Directions:

1. Mix all the ingredients: together thoroughly. Roll the mixture into tiny balls and serve.
2. Delicious dressings

3. Transform meat, salad or vegetable with these lowfat sauces.

Turkey Meatballs Recipe: Dukan Diet Quickstart Guide

Ingredients:

- 1/2 c. nonfat cottage cheese

- 1/4 c. oat bran

- 1/2 c. fresh mint, minced

- 1 tsp. dried oregano

- 680 grams. ground turkey (organic, if possible)

- 1 medium onion, grated

- 2 cloves garlic, minced

- 2 egg whites, beaten

- salt and pepper to taste

Directions:

1. Combine all the Ingredients: in a mediumsized bowl. Do not overmix or your meatballs can become tough.
2. Scoop out one tablespoon of mixture for each meatball and place formed meatballs on a parchment lined baking sheet.
3. Broil meatballs until browned, turning once.

Healthy Flat Bread

Ingredients:

- 2 eggs

- 1 tsp baking powder

- 1 tsp onion powder

- 1 tsp garlic powder

- 1 tsp italian seasoning

- 1 dash of salt and pepper

- 4 tbsp oat bran

- 2 tbsp fat free greek yougurt

- 4 tbsp fat free cream cheese

- 1 dash cheddar, parmesan, or any cheese (optional)

Directions:

1. Mix all ingredients well in a small bowl.
2. Spray olive oil spray lightly to coat bottom of medium small square baking dish.
3. Pour all Ingredients: into baking dish and spread evenly.
4. Microwave for 56 minutes until edges come away from sides.
5. Let cool for 3 minutes.
6. Use spatula to loosen bread. Flip over onto cutting board and let cool for a few more minutes. Cut into 4 squares.
7. Toast 2 pieces at a time in the toaster until lightly browned.

Friendly Turkey Meatballs

Ingredients:

- 2 egg whites (beaten)
- 1/2 cup nonfat ricotta cheese
- 1/4 cup oat bran
- 1/2 tsp dried basil
- 1 1/2 lb organic ground turkey
- 1 medium onion (grated)
- 2 cloves minced garlic
- 1/2 tsp dried oregano

Directions:

1. In a mediumsized bowl, combine all ingredients

2. Scoop out one tablespoon of mixture for and form into round meatballs. Place on a parchment lined baking sheet.
3. Broil meatballs for about ten minutes or until browned, turning once.

Pita According To Dukan

Ingredients:

- 34 tbsp grams of protein isolate (soy or whey)   60 gr

- 3 eggsnot very large

- 180 gr cottage cheesecan be granular or from a pack

- 10 gr baking powder

- Salt

- 2 tbsp cornstarch40 gr(2 DOPs)

- 2 tbsp skimmed milk powder (SOM)30 gr(1DOP)

- 2 tbsp oat bran30 gr

- Any topping suitable for your stage

Directions:

1. For pita, mix all dry Ingredients:.
2. Add to the "drying" eggs and cottage cheese.
3. If the cottage cheese is granular, it is better to punch it with a blender in advance until smooth.
4. Mix the dough until smooth, it is better to do this with a mixer. There should be no lumps of cottage cheese left
5. Leave the dough for 1015 minutes. During this time, it will thicken
6. The dough should be of such a consistency that it does not spread on a baking sheet, does not lose shape
7. If your dough turned out to be watery add a spoonful of isolate or a spoonful of wheat bran, mix and leave the dough to "rest" for another five minutes

8. Now we need to decide what the size of future cakes will be, given that this pita does not increase much when baking.
9. We transfer dough inside a pastry bag (you can take a regular tight bag and cut off a corner)
10. We spread on a silicone mat at a sufficient distance from each other (the pita increases slightly during baking) and form a cake with a wet spoon. A little less than an inch thick.
11. Bake for 2025 minutes at 180° until done. Don't overdry! Pitta puff up and covered with a fragrant crust
12. Remove the finished pita from the mat, put it on the grill
13. IMPORTANT! So that the pita does not dry out! Don't miss the moment when the pitas are barely warm. We put them in a plastic bag and tie them up. In this form, completely cool
14. Now pita is a field for your fantasies!

15. You can cut them with a "pocket", you can cut them in half or lengthwise!
16. We lay out any filling suitable for your stage!
17. I like to warm up readymade pita on the grill, or in the microwave warm it tastes better.
18. Store it in the refrigerator.

Simple Roasted Butternut Squash

Ingredients:

- 2 tablespoons olive oil

- 2 cloves garlic, minced

- 1 butternut squash peeled, seeded, and cut into 1inch cubes

- salt and ground black pepper to taste

Directions:

1. Preheat oven to 400 degrees F (200 degrees C).
2. Toss butternut squash with olive oil and garlic in a large bowl. Season with salt and black pepper. Arrange coated squash on a baking sheet.

3. Roast in the preheated oven until squash is tender and lightly browned, 25 to 30 minutes.

Roast Sticky Chickenrotisserie Style

Ingredients:

- 1 teaspoon white pepper
- ½ teaspoon cayenne pepper
- ½ teaspoon black pepper
- ½ teaspoon garlic powder
- 2 onions, quartered
- 4 teaspoons salt
- 2 teaspoons paprika
- 1 teaspoon onion powder
- 1 teaspoon dried thyme
- 2 (4 pound) whole chickens

Directions:

1. In a small bowl, mix together salt, paprika, onion powder, thyme, white pepper, black pepper, cayenne pepper, and garlic powder.
2. Remove and discard giblets from chicken. Rinse chicken cavity, and pat dry with paper towel. Rub each chicken inside and out with spice mixture.
3. Place 1 onion into the cavity of each chicken. Place chickens in a resealable bag or double wrap with plastic wrap. Refrigerate overnight, or at least 4 to 6 hours.
4. Preheat oven to 250 degrees F (120 degrees C).
5. Place chickens in a roasting pan. Bake uncovered for 5 hours, to a minimum internal temperature of 180 degrees F (85 degrees C). Let the chickens stand for 10 minutes before carving.

Barbara's Sesame Chicken

Ingredients:

- 1/3 cup of Low Sodium Soy Sauce

- 1 tablespoon of Splenda Brown Sugar (The sweetener used by Barbara contains some calories so is best avoided. Try replacing with Splenda no calorie granulated sweetener instead.)

- 1 tablespoon of toasted Sesame Seeds

- 3 Chicken Breasts

- 5 tablespoons of Oat Bran

- Salt and Freshly Ground Black Pepper to taste

Directions:

1. Cut up the chicken breasts.

2. Place the oat bran, salt and pepper in a bag and shake well.
3. Put the pieces of chicken in the bag and shake well again to cover the chicken.
4. Remove the chicken from the bag and dry fry in a pan for about 15 minutes.
5. Take the chicken out of the pan and keep warm.
6. Put the soy sauce and Splenda in the pan and cook for a few minutes.
7. Add the sesame seeds and then the chicken pieces and serve.

Turkey Burgers

Ingredients:

- 1/2 onion
- 1 egg white
- grams of lean turkey mince
- Salt and pepper

Directions:

1. Chop the onion very finely.
2. Place the turkey and onion in a bowl, add a little salt and pepper and mix well.
3. Add the egg white and mix again.
4. Divide the mixture in two and form two burgers.
5. Dry fry in a nonstick pan turning once halfway through cooking.

Basil Pesto Artichokes

Ingredients:

- 3 tbsp basil pesto

- 4 tbsp olive oil

- 2 tbsp finely chopped garlic

- 4 medium artichokes

Directions:

1. Bring an inch of water to a boil in a large pot. Make sure a steamer basket can fit into the pot without touching the water.
2. Meanwhile, prepare artichokes remove stems and the lower, small leaves. Slice off the top of the artichokes, around an inch down.
3. Place artichokes into a steamer basket, and steam for 15 minutes.

4. In a small skillet, heat oil, and fry garlic until lightly browned. Then, add pesto, and cook until heated through remove from fire.
5. Artichokes are cooked when the stem is soft. Transfer to a serving plate, and position artichokes upright, as you evenly pour the oil and pesto mixture over them, ensuring that you fill each nook and cranny with the sauce.
6. Serve, and enjoy!

Sautéed Shiitake And Swiss Chard

Ingredients:

- 4 caps of shiitake mushrooms

- 4 tbsp unsalted butter

- 1 tsp fresh thyme leaves

- 9 oz Swiss chard, thinly sliced crosswise

Directions:

1. Thoroughly wash chopped swiss chard until clean, and dry thoroughly.
2. On mediumhigh fire, place skillet, and heat 2 tbsp butter. Add thyme and mushroom. Season with salt, and cook for a minute, or until fragrant.

3. Lessen the heat, and add chard. Gently sauté occasionally, and cook for 4 minutes, or until chard has wilted.
4. Bring fire back to mediumhigh, and continue cooking for 3 minutes, or until liquid has evaporated.
5. Add the remaining butter, and cook for 3 minutes more.
6. Remove from fire, transfer to a serving dish, and season with pepper and salt before serving.

Cheese And Garlic Chicken Pocket

Ingredients:

- 4 tbsp. of sans fat cream cheese
- Garlic powder, as desired
- 2 bosoms of chicken
- Salt, genuine, as desired

Directions:

1. Preheat broiler to 350F.
2. Slice chicken bosoms in center region. Make pockets. Don't slice totally through.
3. Sprinkle garlic powder and fit salt as wanted inside pockets made in sync
4. Spread aluminum foil in cooking plate. It ought to be of adequate size to put chicken bosoms inside and wrap meat.

5. Place 1 to 2 tbsp. of cream cheddar in pockets. Add extra garlic powder, whenever wanted. Seal meat up utilizing your fingers. Sprinkle parsley over the top.
6. Cover all with foil and close it up. Cook in 350F broiler for 1/2 hour.
7. Open foil. Set broiler to barbecue. Cook for 10 to 15 additional minutes and serve.

Pink Cheesecake Cupcake

Ingredients:

- 4 oz lowfat sour cream (for frosting)

- 24 packets or 1 cup Splenda (1/2 for cupcake, 1/2 for frosting)

- 1 tspn vanilla extract (1/2 for each)

- 4 oz fatfree cream cheese

- 2 eggs

- 1 egg white

- .51 drop of red food coloring

Directions:

1. Blend cream cheese and 1/2 Splenda. Slowly add in eggs. Portion to cupcake tin. Bake @

350 for ~30 minutes. Remove and allow to cool.
2. Blend sour cream and other 1/2 of Splenda. Add vanilla and if desired, 1 drop of red food coloring.
3. Dollop on top, cook for another 57 minutes. Allow to cool.

Lemon Chicken Light

Ingredients:

- 3 bonein chicken breasts, skin removed (reduce cooking time if using boneless breasts) (The chicken breasts I bought were huge, so I cut each in half to make 6 servings.)

- 2 c. lemon juice (preferably fresh squeezed, but bottled is fine)

- 2 T. oat bran, ground in food processor or coffee grinder

- 1 t. paprika

- Dash of salt and pepper

- 1/2 package of Crystal Light Lemonade Powder Mix (makes 8 servings if prepared according to package)

- 1 T. Chicken Flavor Better Than Bouillion Paste
- 1/2 tsp. lemon extract
- 1 whole lemon

Directions:

1. Place chicken breasts in glass container then pour over lemon juice. Make sure all the pieces are just submerged. Refrigerate overnight.
2. Mix together ground oat bran, paprika, salt, pepper, and Crystal Light Mix in large bowl.
3. Drain chicken, but keep 3 oz. (6 T.) of the lemon juice marinade. Pat chicken dry with paper towel.
4. Dredge each piece in oat bran mixture, then place in baking pan just large enough to hold the pieces without overlapping.
5. Mix together the reserved lemon juice, the boullion paste, and lemon extract.

6. Pour over chicken pieces. Slice the whole lemon thin, and place the slices over the pieces, then bake at 375 about 45 minutes or until the chicken is done (juices are clear when pierced with a fork and no pink remains at the bone.) This is terrific hot or cold!

Sticky Chicken

Ingredients:

- 3 tbsp. Soy sauce, low sodium

- 3 tbsp. Vinegar, balsamic

- 2 tsp. Chili paste

- 8 chicken tenders, boneless and skinless

- 1 tsp. Splenda

Directions:

1. Brown each side of chicken pieces in skillet presprayed with nonstick spray. Thighs will usually take about five minutes per side, and tenders will often be done in three minutes per side.

2. Combine remainder of Ingredients: in sauce pan. Bring to boil. Simmer for five minutes. Mixture should have thickened.
3. After chicken is browned, add sauce to skillet. Cook for about five to 10 minutes for chicken thighs or five to seven minutes for chicken tenders. Serve.

www.ingramcontent.com/pod-product-compliance
Lightning Source LLC
LaVergne TN
LVHW010226070526
838199LV00062B/4735